To:	Whom it may concern
Cc...	Big Boss
Subject:	What my emails really mean!

"as per my last email"

Add some excitement to your desk as you translate your " polite" emails into what you really mean!

Kind Regards, (kindly get screwed),

GW00514924

"Moving Forward"

Please just let it go already!

"I'll let you know as soon as I hear anything"

Please forget already! I definitely won't be replying back to you.

"Thanks in advance"

You **WILL** do this favour for me, I've already thanked you for it!

"Sorry for being unclear"

Obviously you didn't really read what I wrote!

"Just checking in"

Just answer my damn email!

"Just a friendly reminder"

Don't you dare forget! I've reminded you more than enough times!

"If you have further questions, please do not hesitate to ask"

DO NOT ask me any more stupid questions on this matter!

"Looking forward to your thoughts"

You'd better agree with me, asshole!

"Kind Regards"

Now, kindly get screwed!

"Please advise me"

I really have no idea! Save me!

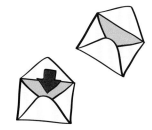

"As per my last email"

MESSAGE

Can't you read? Stop asking stupid questions and just read the damn thing again!

"I'll get this to you shortly"

It's the least of my worries, have you seen my damned workload?

"Quick question"

Give me a quick reply! I haven't got all day!

"Thank you"

Screw you!

MESSAGE

"I hope you're well"

I really don't care, but I really need to be nice before I ask you this hellish request!

"I've cc'd _the Boss_ just to keep them in the loop"-

I've alerted them to your total cock up! You're definitely screwed now!

"As promised"

Here you go, stop your whining now you insufferable pain in the ass!

"To re-iterate"

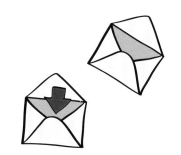

This is the last time I'm saying this! Don't ask again!

"I see your point"

You can express your opinion but I don't give a damn! ↗

"As stated below"

You need to read the entire chain, not just the top two lines because your dumb question has already been answered!

"Let me clarify"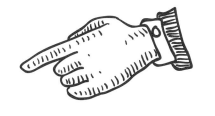

You completely misunderstood my last message, you idiot!

"Hope this helps"

Just stop bothering me!

"I'll let you two take it from here"

I'm not part of this and don't want to be!

"As previously discussed"

I didn't put it in writing last time because I thought you were an adult!

"Just circling back on this"

I just need an answer, A god damn "yes" or "no" will do, *just answer!*

"Could you provide a little more detail?"

Whatever you tried to say makes absolutely no god damn sense!

"Thanks for the input!"

Don't speak to me again ever!

"Just so I understand"

What you are saying is so unacceptable that I am going to make you repeat it!

"Please copy everyone on our team"

Stop sending work requests to me alone on my day off!

"I recall this quite differently"

You're a bald, two-faced liar and snake!

"To put it more simply"

Are you seriously that stupid?

"Not sure if my last email was received"

Just how long do think you can ignore me?

MESSAGE

"Would you like me to forward it back to you?"

We both know you were sent the original message. Don't make me pull receipts!

"Correct me if I'm wrong"

I know I'm not wrong and there is no use in trying to challenge my opinion!

MAIL

"In case you missed it"

You're not doing what I said you should be doing. Do I really need to repeat myself?

"As you are no doubt aware"

We both know you are aware of it, stop pretending to be an idiot!

"With respect"

I don't give a crap how important you **THINK** you are, you're wrong and this needs to happen!

"Great!"

It's far from great but there's nothing I can do about it!

"Please advise"

What the hell? Stop wasting my time and do your job!

"Going forward"

I can't move on without casually reminding you that you messed up **BIG TIME**, so don't do it again!

"Let me know if you have any concerns"

You better have no more questions as I don't have any answers.

"Just wanted to touch base with you on____"

You're taking far too damn long!

"In order to set expectations"

Let me tell you what is not going to happen...

"Happy to discuss"

Everyone just leave me alone!